WORDS

MICHAEL PAUSE

IN *ACTION*

ACTION

TION

ION

ON

N

SEEING THE MEANING OF WORDS

How often do you think about words?

Maybe all the time, maybe never. But words are the basis of language. They are the building blocks of communication.

Words in Action is the result of my thinking about words over many years. The concepts that underpin the visual "words" in this book are found in, and build upon, *Watching Words Move*, the groundbreaking book created by Ivan Chermayeff and Tom Geismar in 1962. In the late 1950s these two graphic designers, who were interested in the visual world of print and typography, set out in a disciplined way to express the meaning of words using one size of only one font, with related characters, punctuation, symbols, and abbreviations. The surprising results—words arranged to show what they mean—forever changed the way graphic artists thought about words' graphic potential.

The works of three earlier creative individuals stand out as stimuli for Chermayeff and Geismar. First is Guillaume Apollinaire (1880–1918), a French poet who produced a series of calligrams, or poems whose words are shaped into images that relate to the meaning of the poem. A poem about the Eiffel Tower, for example, would be arranged into the shape of the famous landmark. In his 1918 book *Caligrammes*, the words of poems are arranged into images of a horse, a palm tree, an open book, a woman's torso, and a building—all of which add to the meaning of the textual and visual compositions.

Next is the Italian poet Filippo Tommaso Marinetti (1876–1944), best known as the founder of Futurism. His 1919 book *Les mots en liberté futuristes* (Futurist Words in Freedom) added to the ideas of experimental typography and visual poetry. Its pages display type of different fonts and weights dynamically arranged by Marinetti to create graphic images that look like abstract drawings. He ignored traditional rules of syntax and punctuation, producing a visual idea of modern life that inspired many other Futurist artists.

The third artist known for exploring typography as a visual expression is the Romanian-born American illustrator Saul Steinberg (1914–1999). Steinberg's style is easily recognized by the many playful, clever cartoons he published in the *New Yorker*. In one of his witty drawings from 1961, a person sitting behind a desk is saying "NO" to the person seated in front of him. The speech balloon takes the shape of a large NO, its outline filled with elaborate, looping handwriting. Throughout the 1960s, Steinberg created artworks that featured words as the subject, often manipulating letters to portray meanings and express ideas.

Words in Action is inspired by these earlier generations, especially Chermayeff and Geisner. Not wanting to be as structured, and thus restricted, as they were,

I started with a broader palette of fonts, sizes, and manipulations of the type. After some initial designs, life took over and the effort went dormant. Occasionally one or two or ten new words would reengage my interest in the project, but then another quiet period would follow. It was a process that had a life of its own. Finally, my practice resulted in the inventory that is shown on these pages, a portfolio that adds to the collection first published in *Watching Words Move*.

Just as *Watching Words Move* served as a catalyst for me, so can *Words in Action* stimulate you to look at the ordinary in an out-of-the-ordinary creative way.

WORDS IN *ACTION*

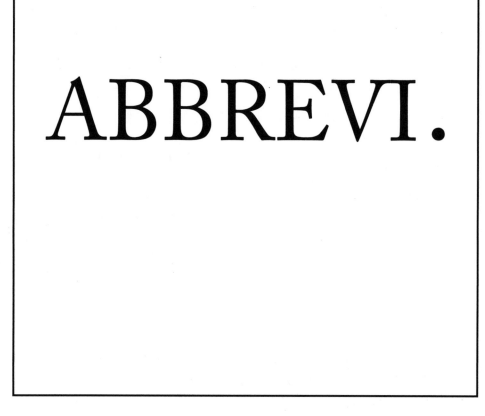

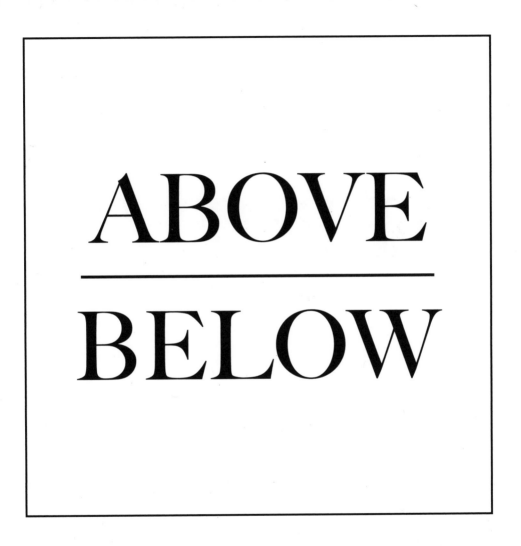

ACCURATE

UNACCURATE

ACHROMATIC

Alphanumeric

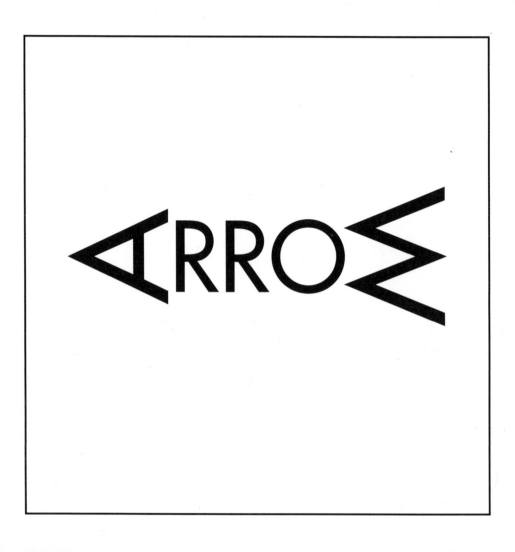

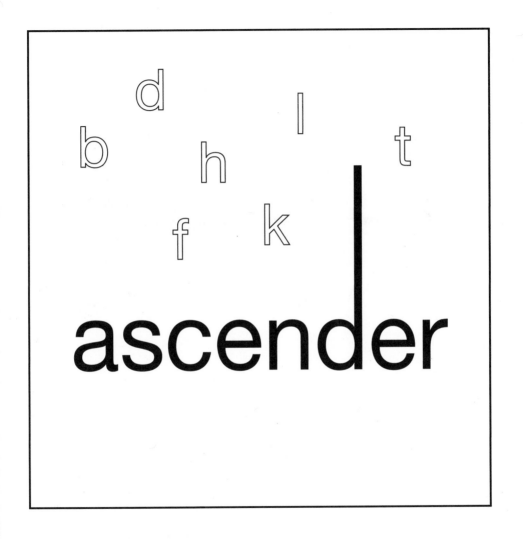

ascender

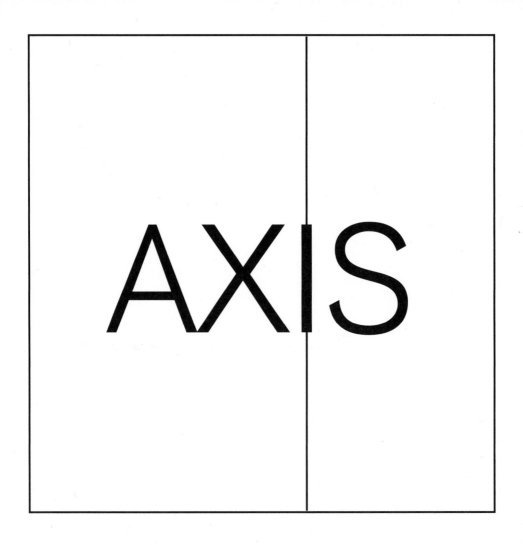

BACKWARD

DRAWKCAB

BEFORE *between* after

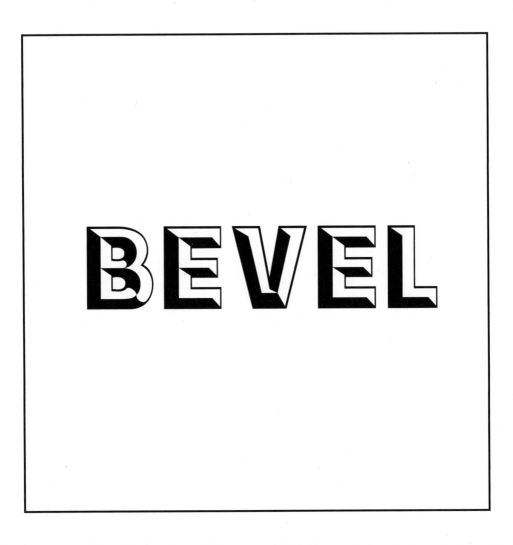

SMALL

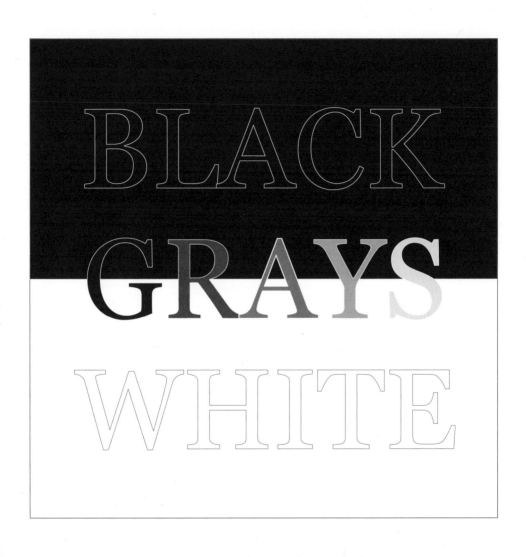

BORDER BORDER BORDER BORDER BORDER BORDER
BORDER BORDER BORDER BORDER BORDER BORDER BORDER
BORDER BORDER BORDER BORDER BORDER BORDER BORDER
BORDER BORDER BORDER BORDER BORDER BORDER BORDER

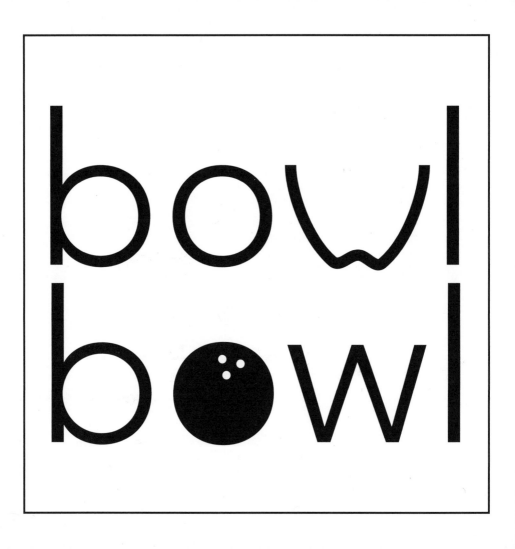

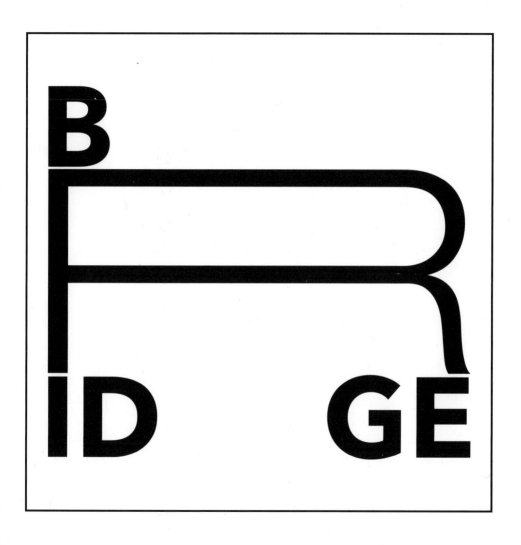

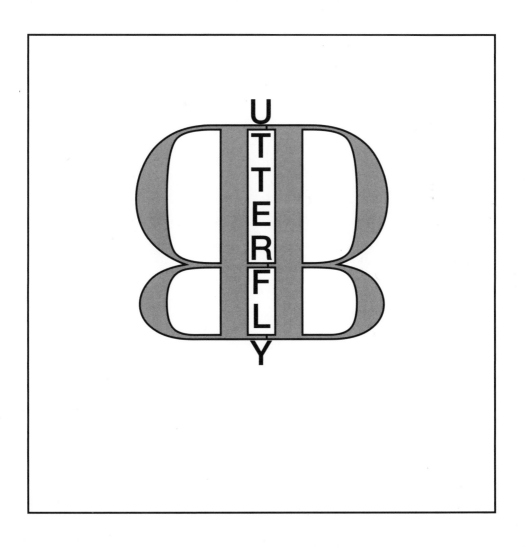

CALLIGRAPHY

CANTILEVER

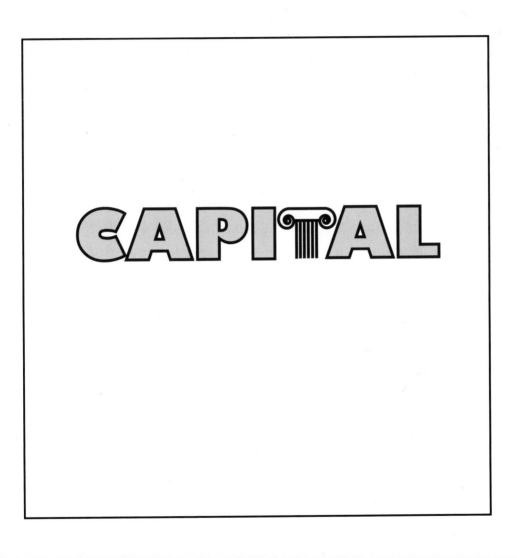

Captive

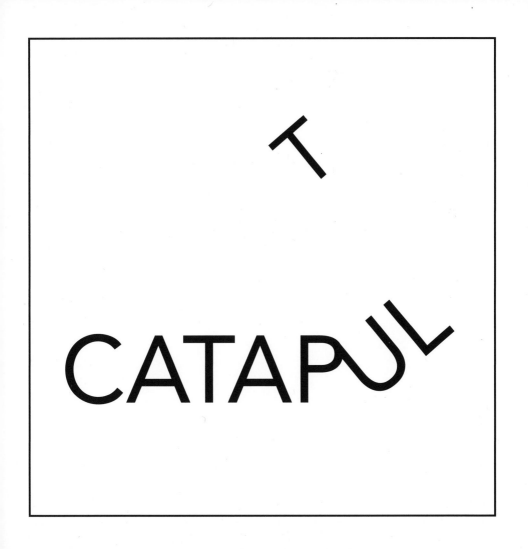

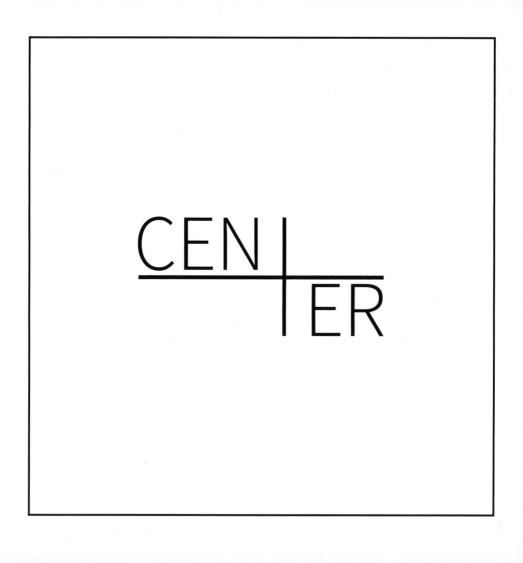

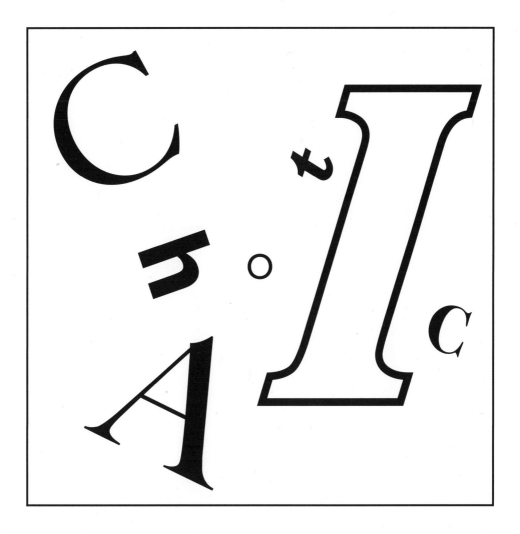

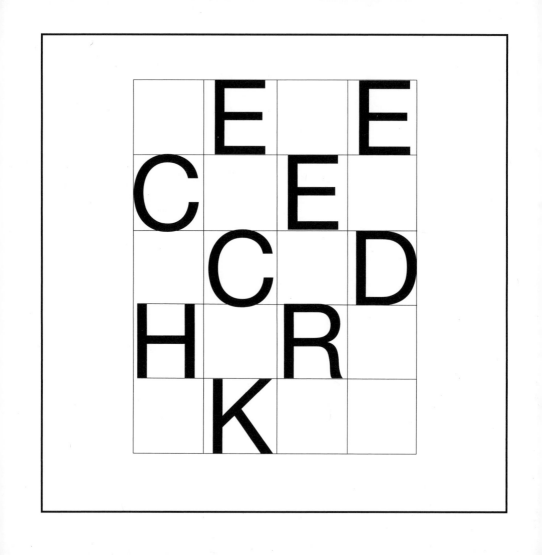

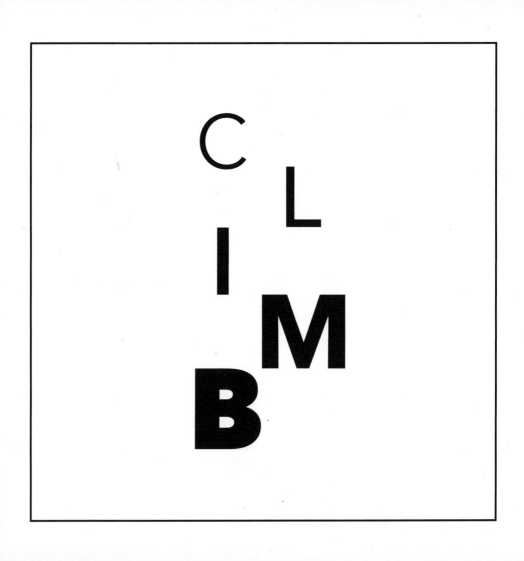

CLUSTER

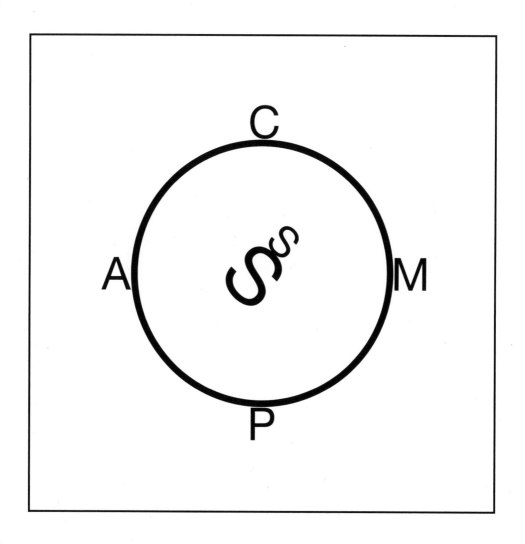

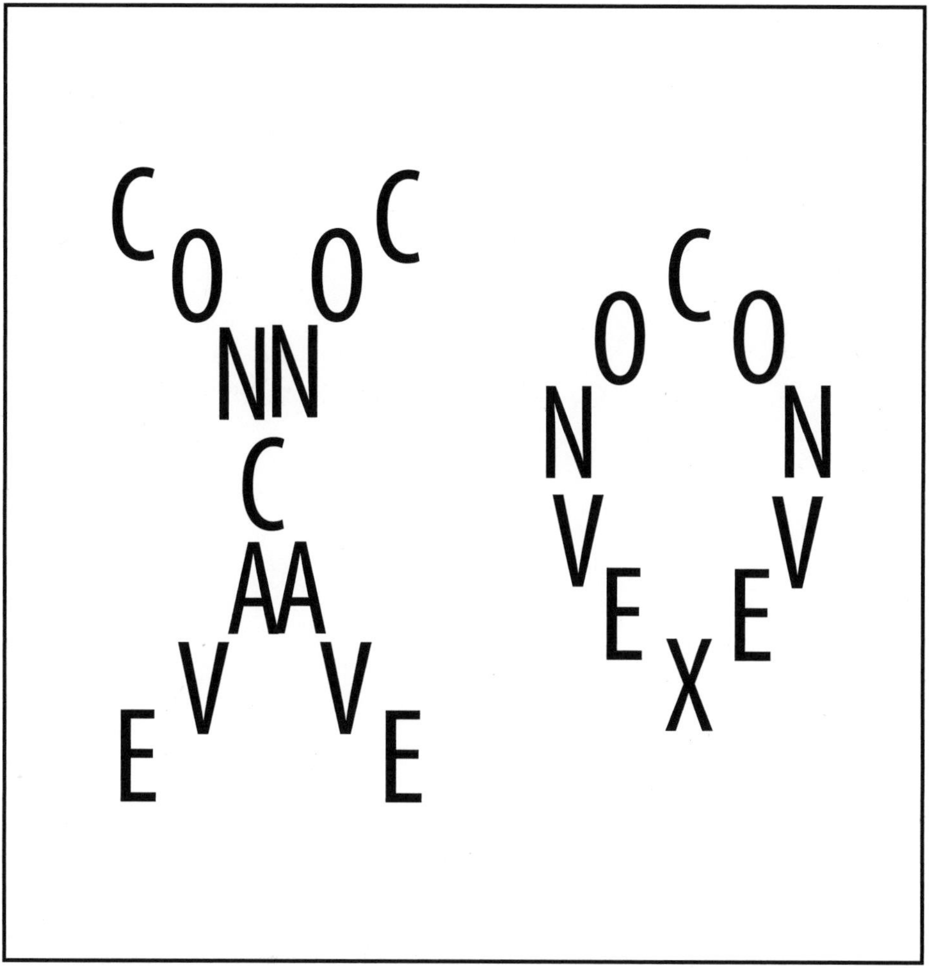
CONCAVE
CONVEX

Confiscate

CONSTRICT

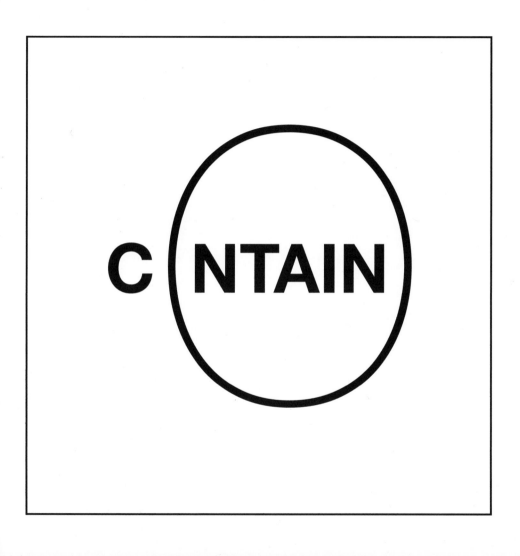

CONTIGUOUS

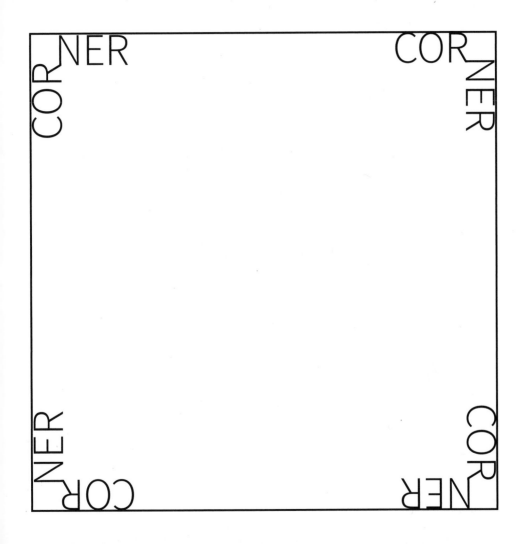

CORRECT
INCORECT

RIGHT
RONG

ERRORR

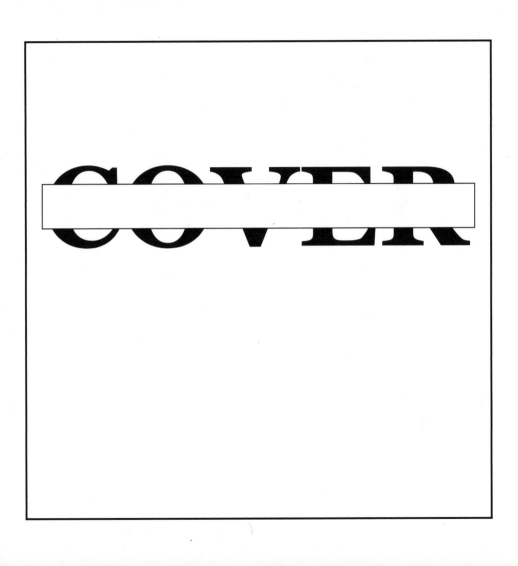

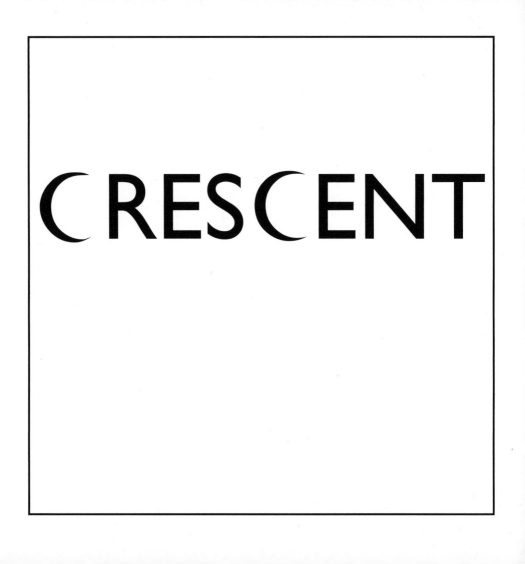
CRESCENT

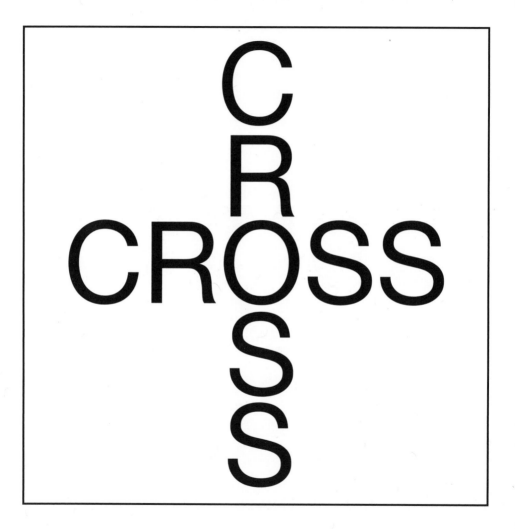

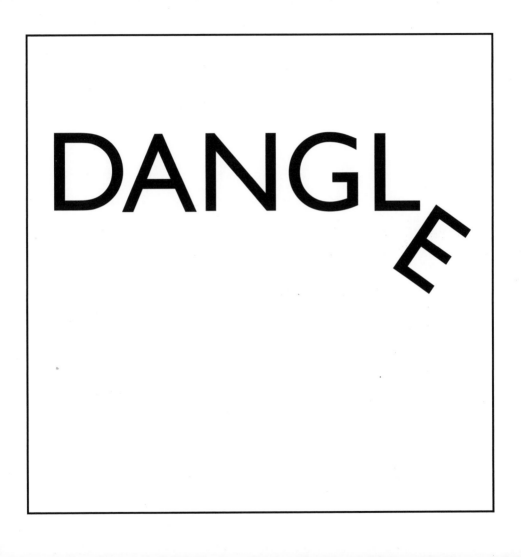

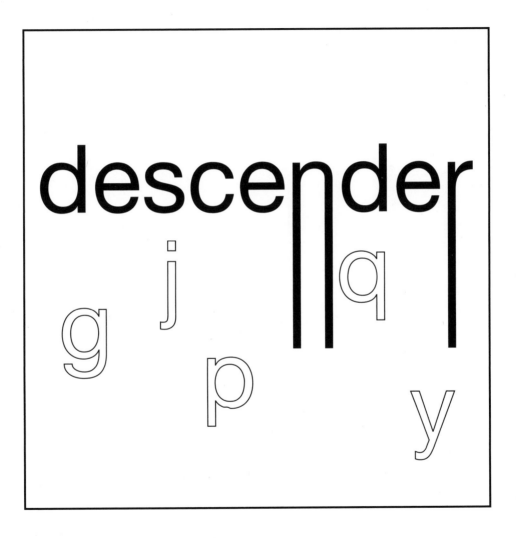

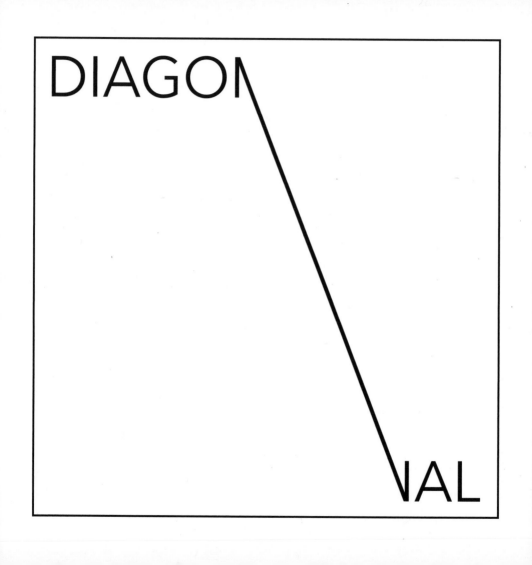

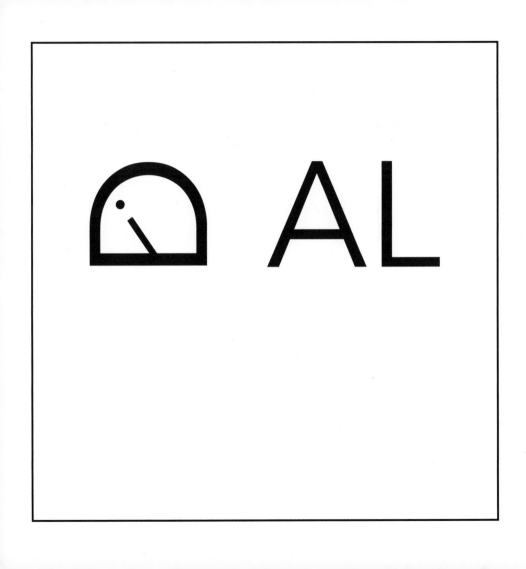

dIfFeReNt

DIssIMILAR

DIGRA*PH*

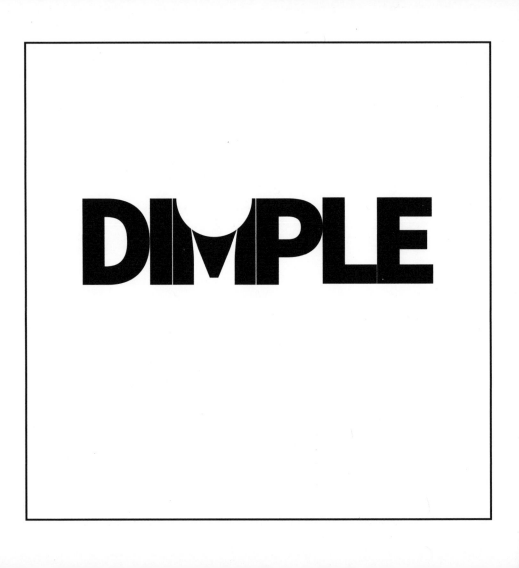

DISASSEMBLE

DISAPPEA

DISCREPANSY

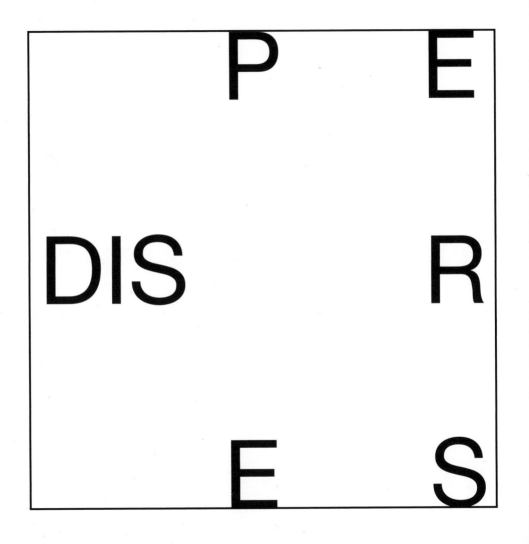

DISPR∘P O RTI∘NATE

dissociate

••

$$\frac{\text{DIVIDEND}}{\text{DIVISOR}}$$

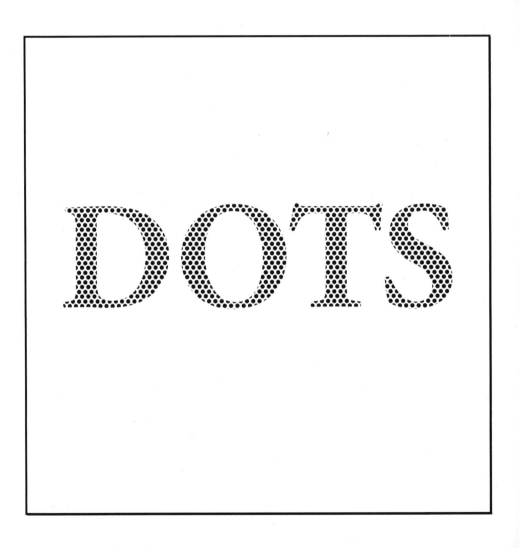

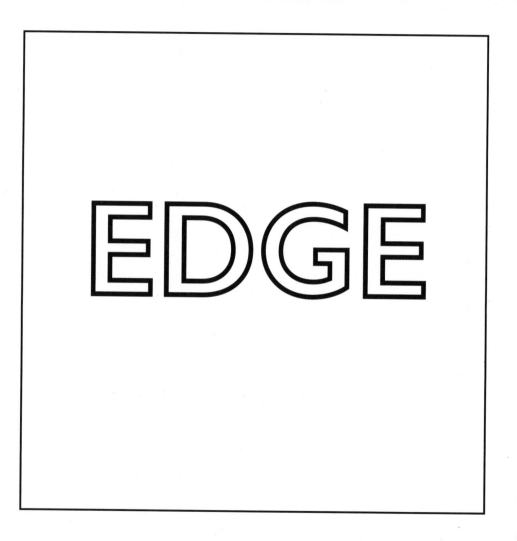

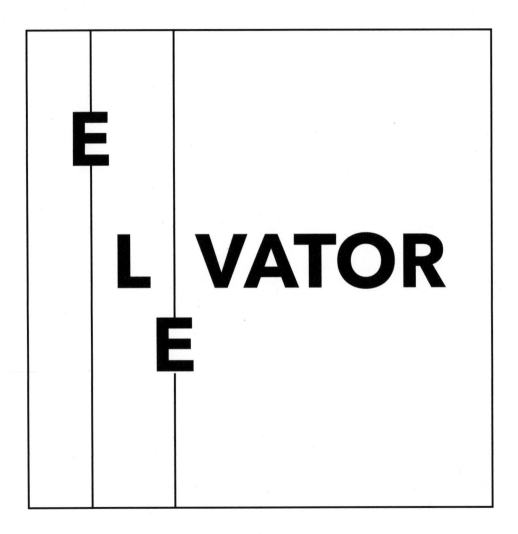

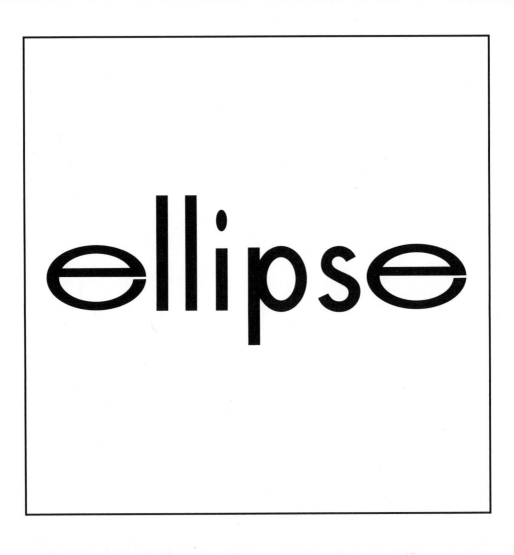

empty

fill

full

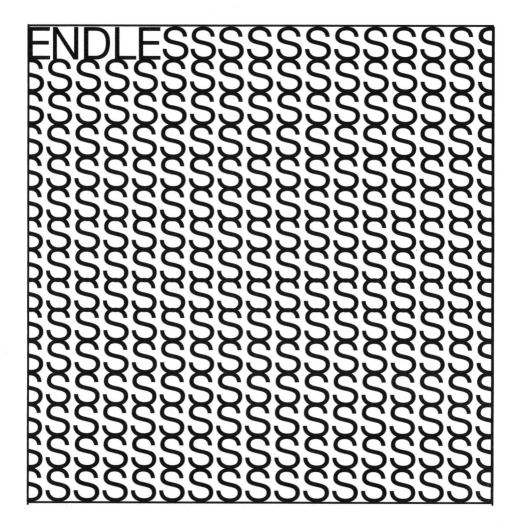

EQUIL△TER△L

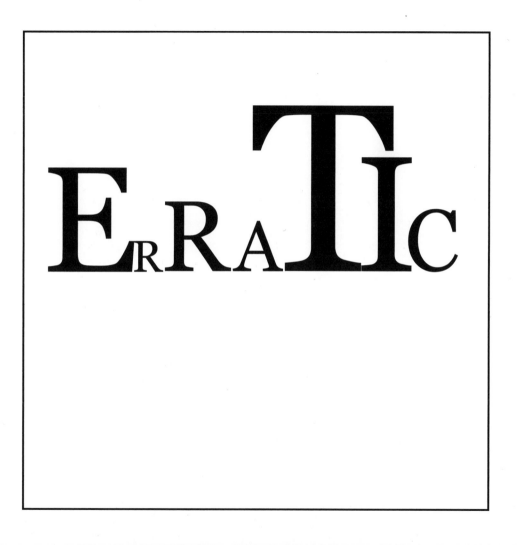

exc!a!m

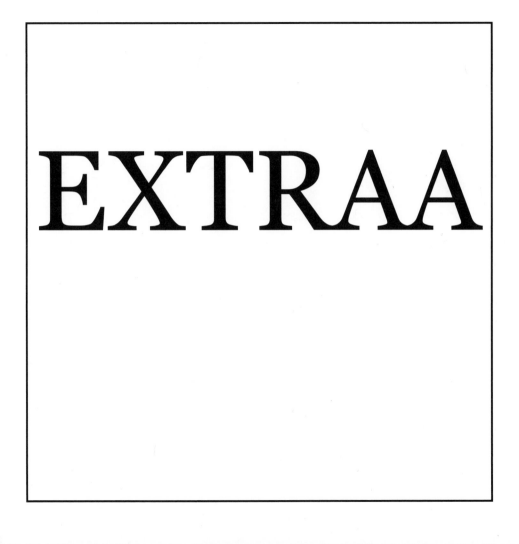

EXTRAA

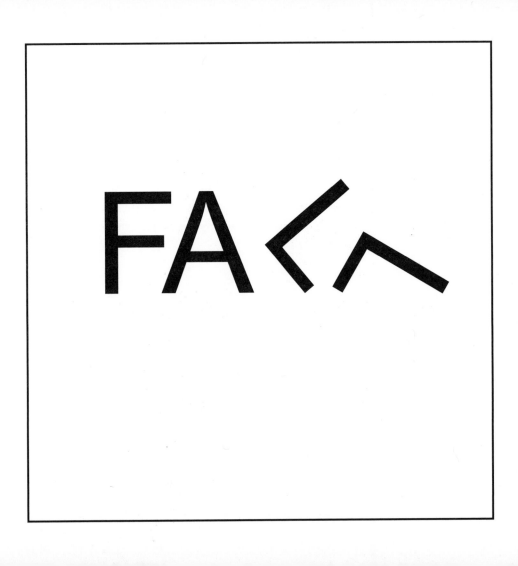

FIS SURE

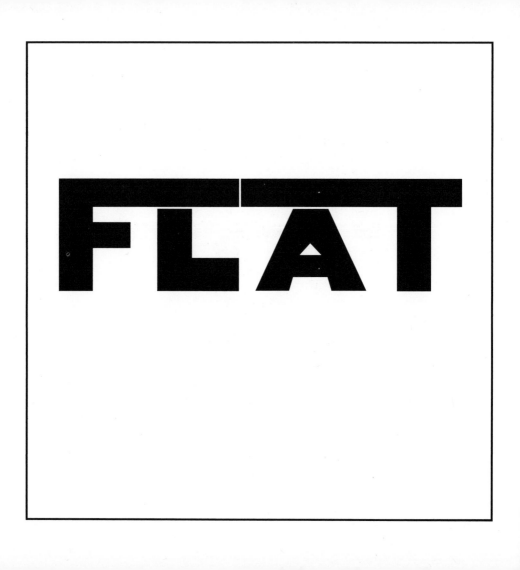

FRAGMENT

GRADATION

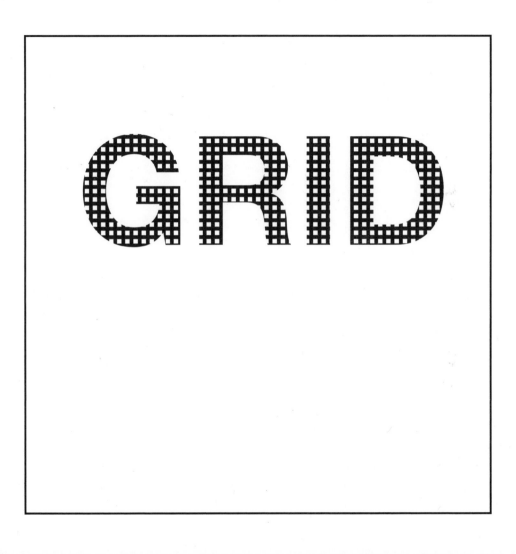

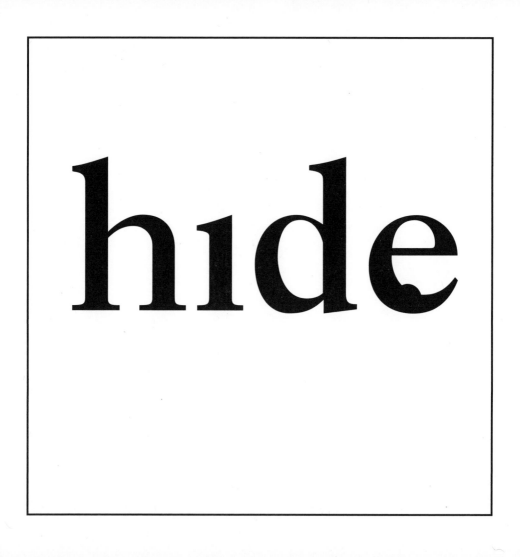

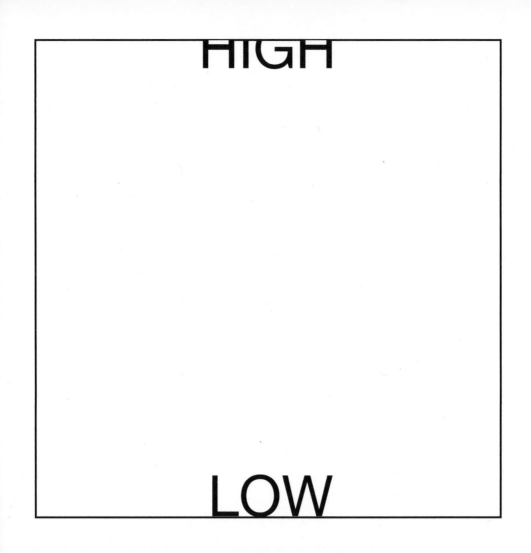

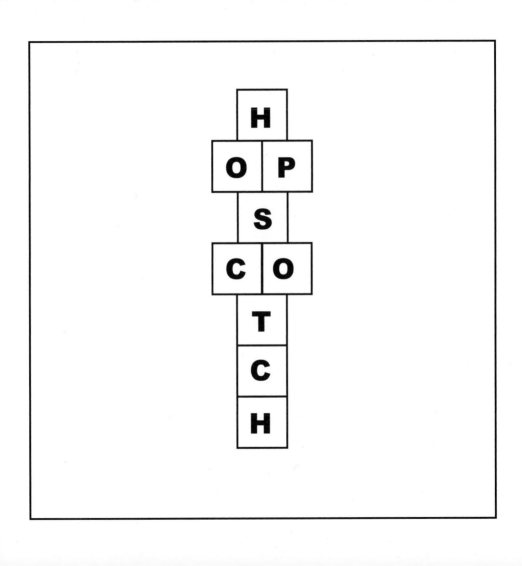

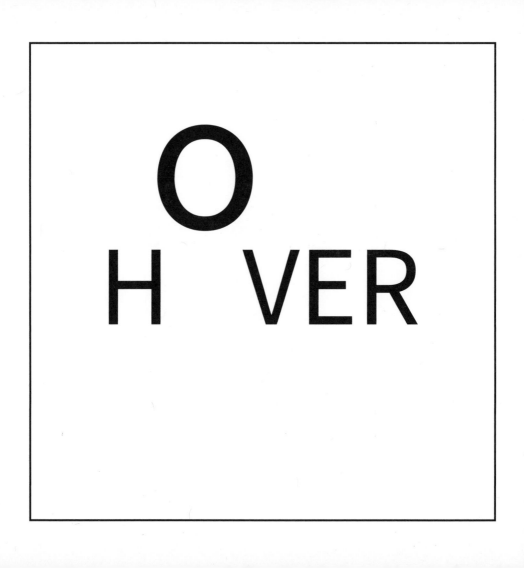

hy-phen-ate

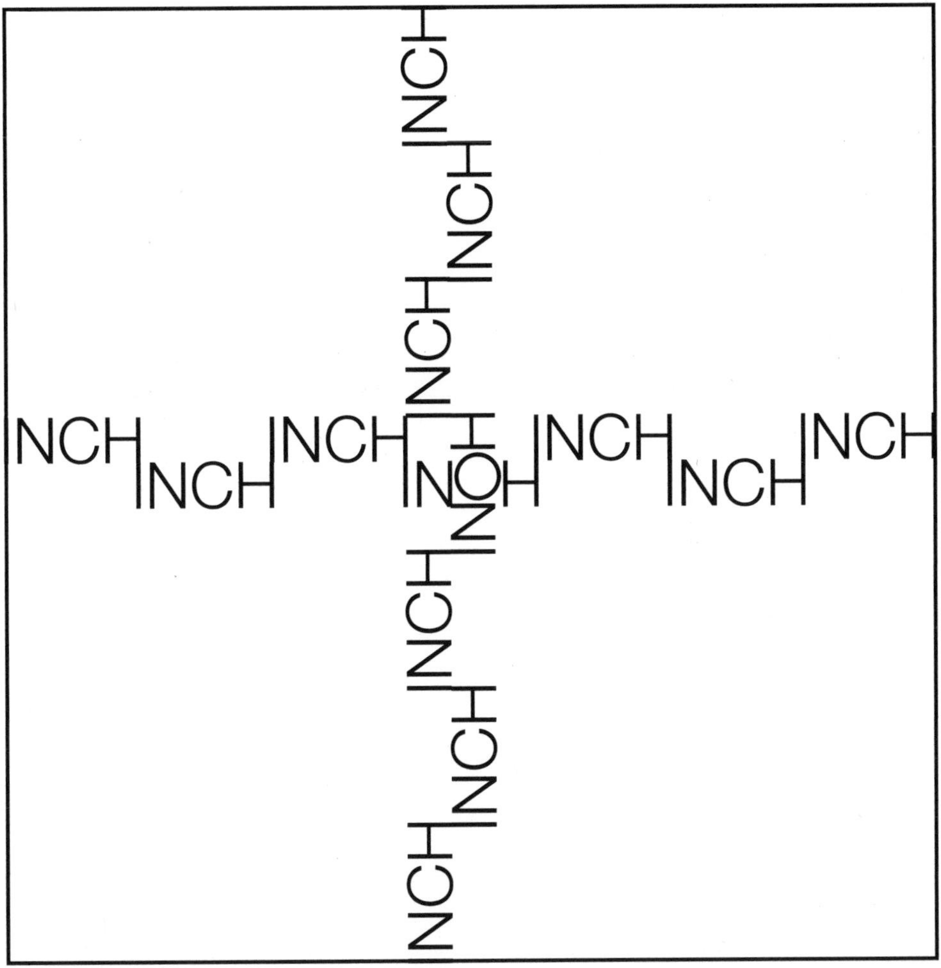
INCH INCH INCH INCH INCH INCH INCH

INCOMPLE

INDICATE

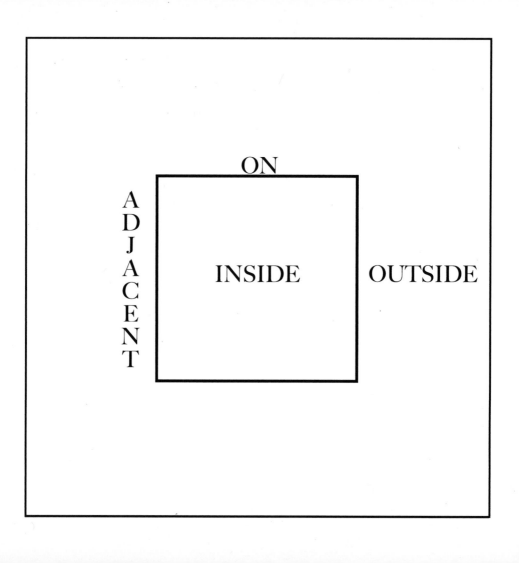

INSIGINIFICANT * SMALL* MICROSCOPIC * MINATURE * MINUSCULE * TINY
MINIMUM * INFINITESMAL * LITTLE * MINUTE * NEGLIGIBLE * DIMINUTIVE
LIMITED * PALTRY * SLIGHT * MINI * INADEQUATE * LIMITED *MINIMAL * BIT

I·N·T·E·R·S·P·E·R·S·E

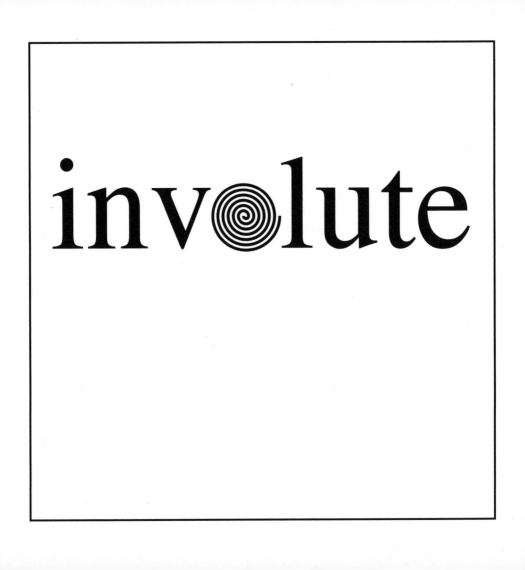

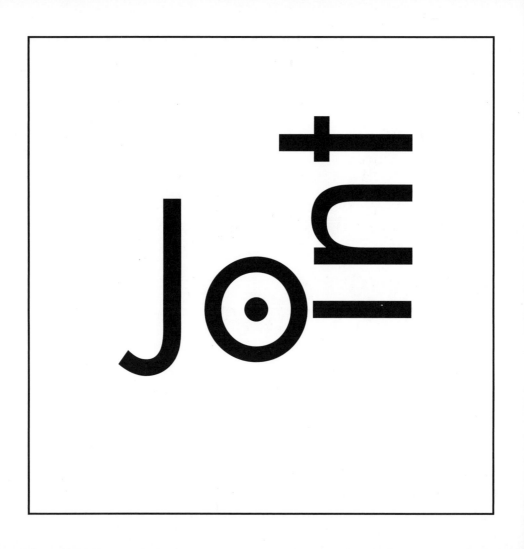

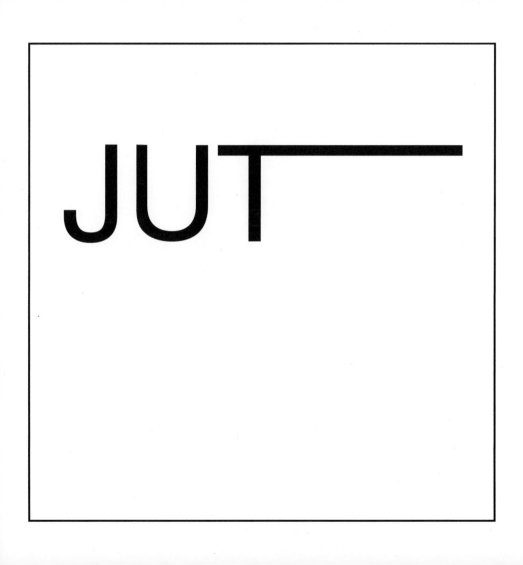

LATITUDE LATITUDE

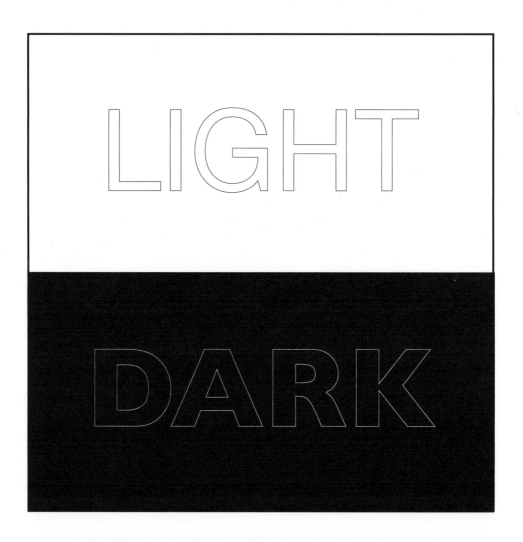

LINEAR

PLANAR

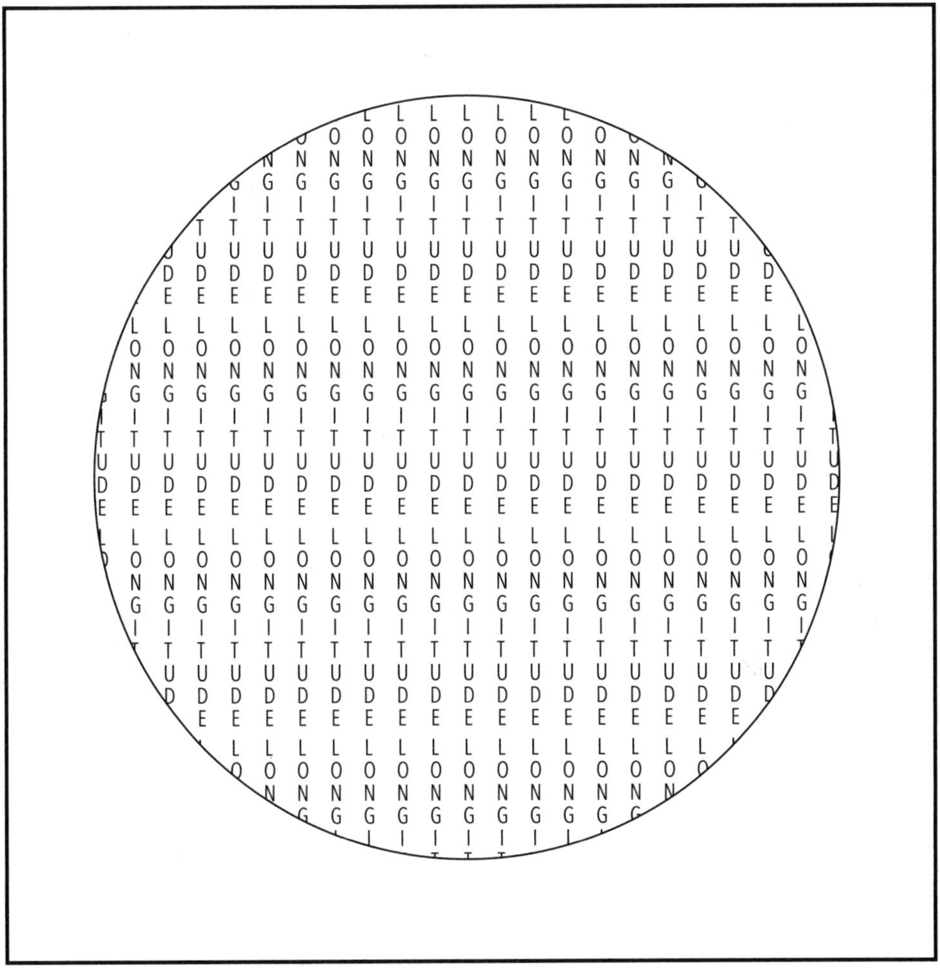
LONGITUDE

MANY MANY MANY MANY MANY MANY MANY
MANY MANY MANY MANY MANY MANY MANY
MANY MANY MANY MANY MANY MANY MANY
MANY MANY MANY MANY MANY MANY MANY
MANY MANY MANY MANY MANY MANY MANY
MANY MANY MANY MANY MANY MANY MANY
MANY MANY MANY MANY MANY MANY MANY
MANY MANY MANY MANY MANY MANY MANY
MANY MANY MANY MANY MANY MANY MANY
MANY MANY MANY MANY MANY MANY MANY
MANY MANY MANY MANY MANY MANY MANY
MANY MANY MANY MANY MANY MANY MANY
MANY MANY MANY MANY MANY MANY MANY
MANY MANY MANY MANY MANY MANY MANY
MANY MANY MANY MANY MANY MANY MANY

FEW   FEW   FEW

meander

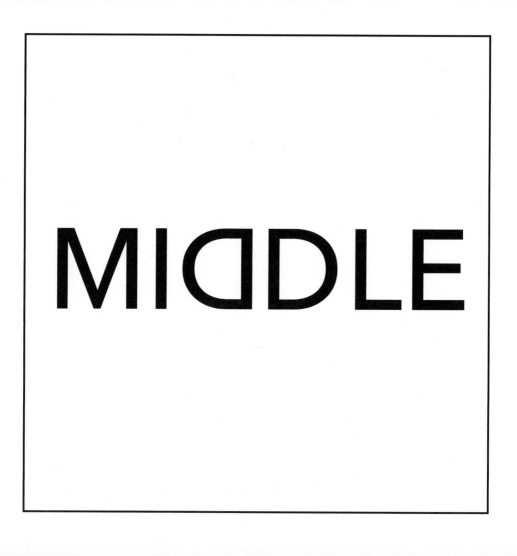

mlspiace

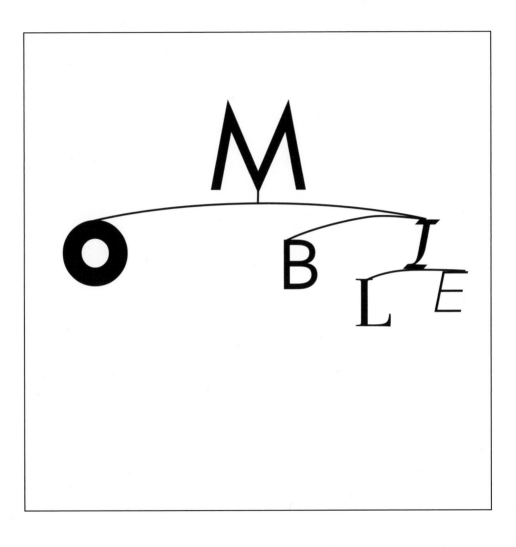

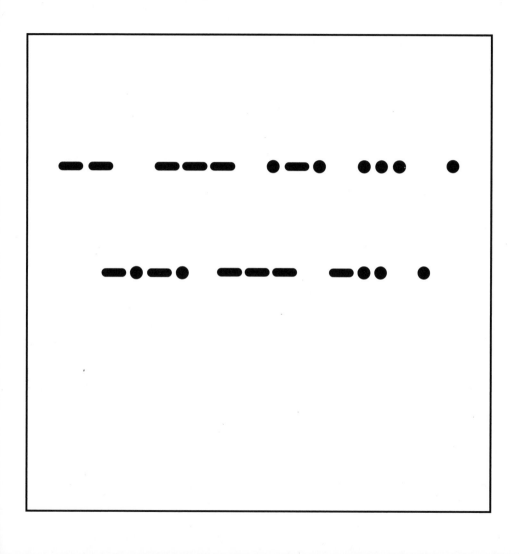

MM UU LL TT II PP LL EE
MM UU LL TT II PP LL EE
MM UU LL TT II PP LL EE

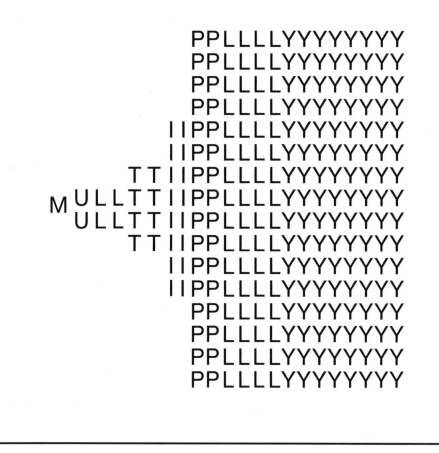

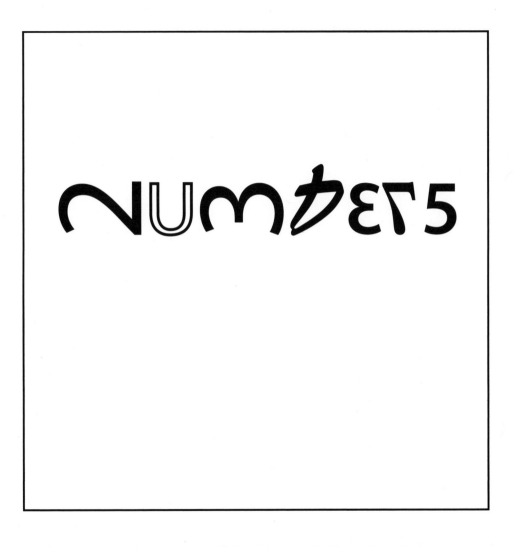

OBSOLETE

MODERN

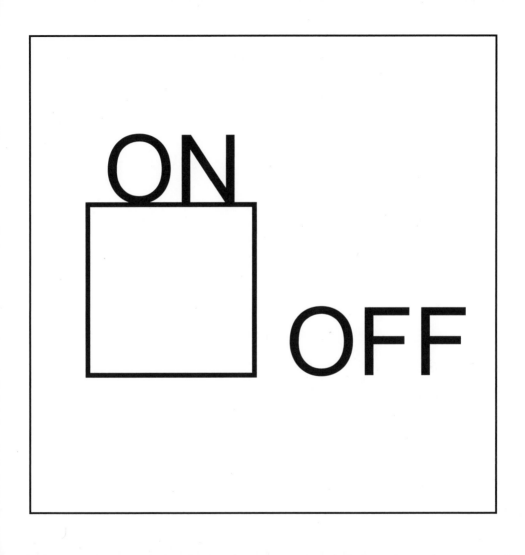

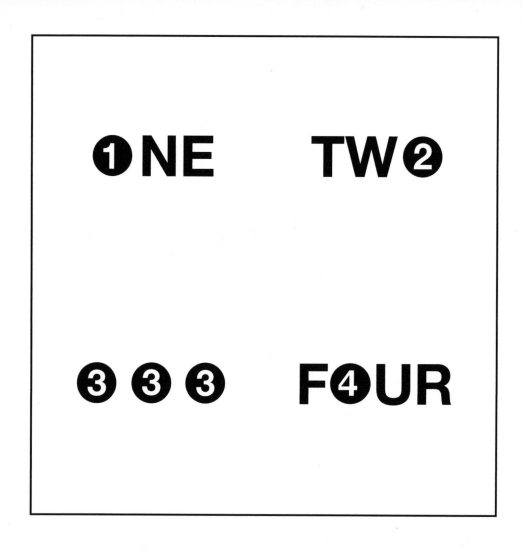

ORIENTATION

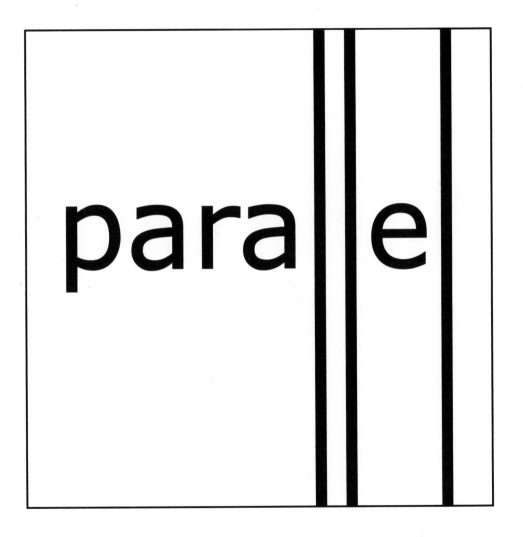

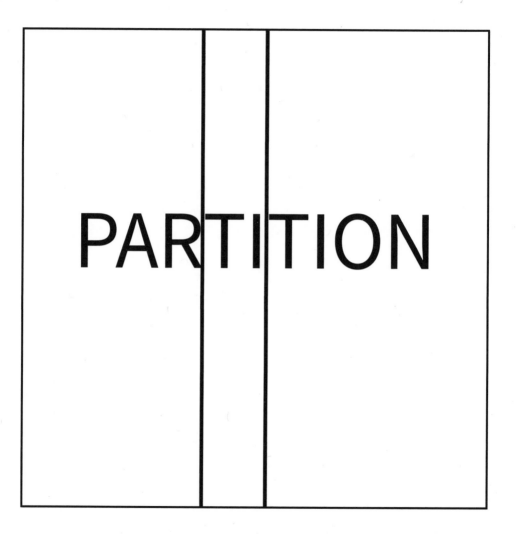

PENTAG⬠N

HEXAG⬡N

⬡CTAG⬡N

PERFORATE

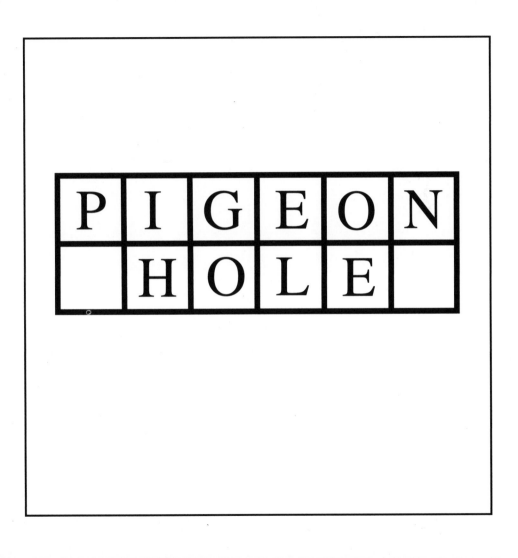

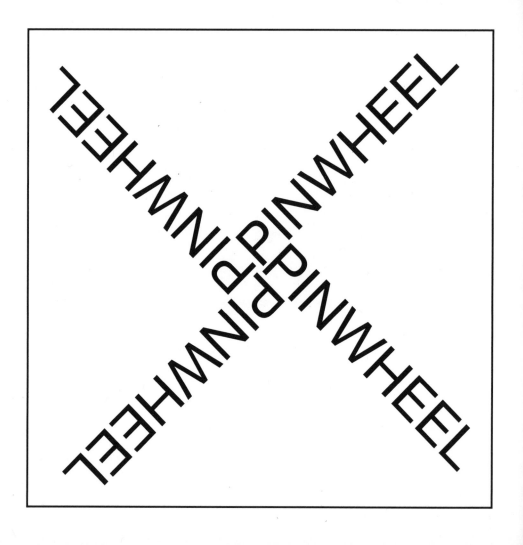

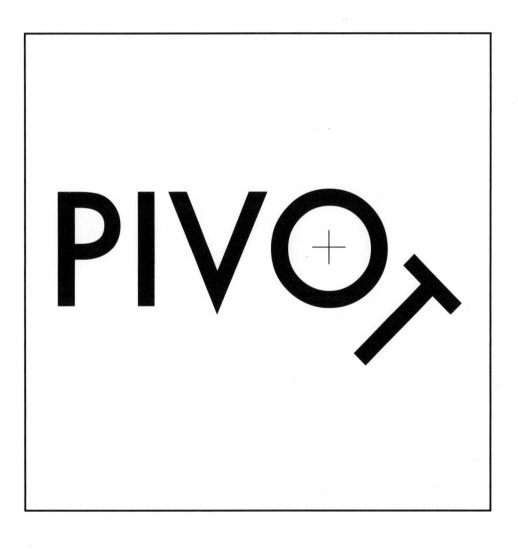

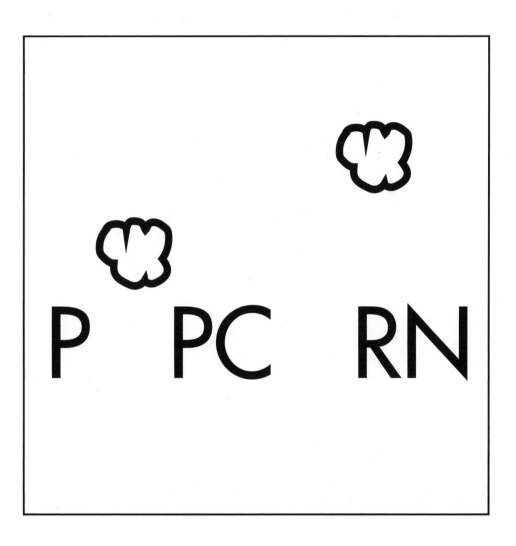

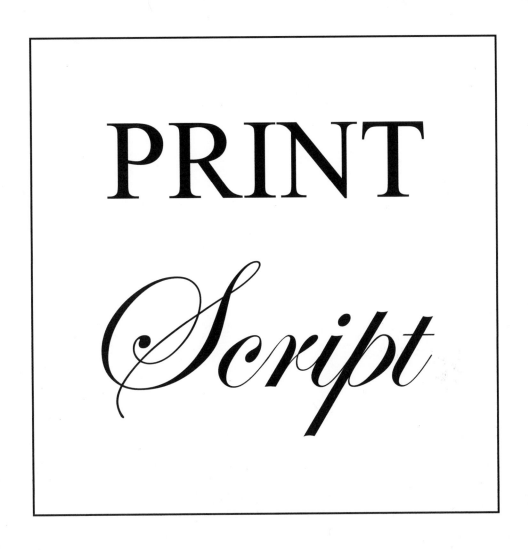

PROGRESSION

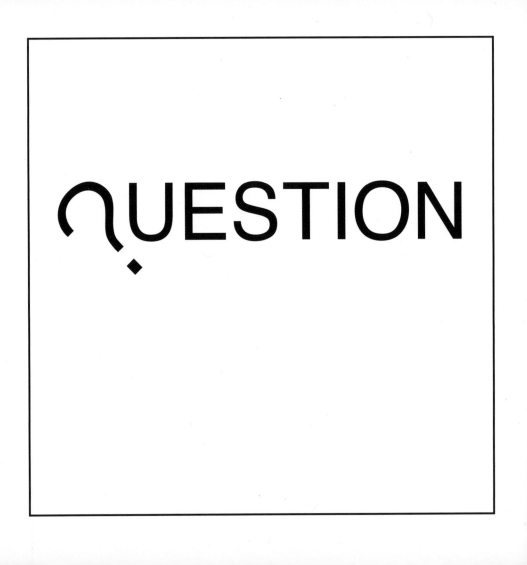

QUICKSAND

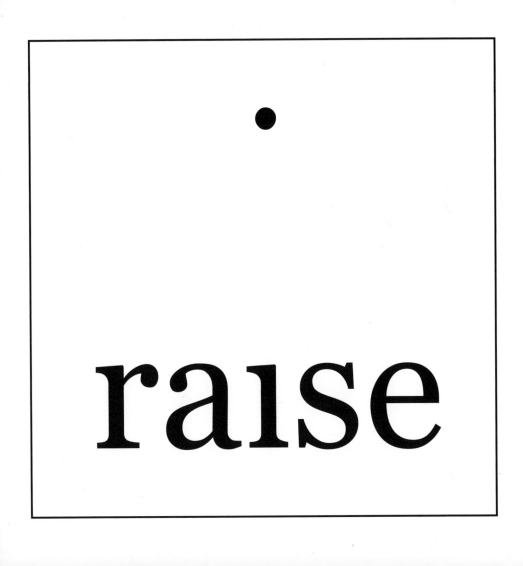

raise

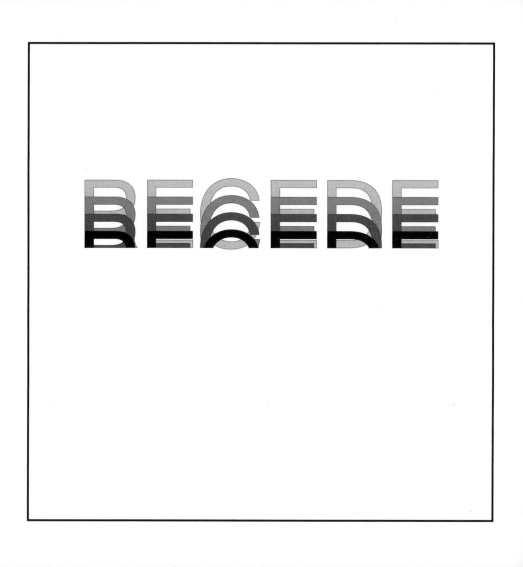

RECESS

REFLECTT

REPETITIVE REPETITIVE REPETITIVE REPETITIVE REPETITIVE
REPETITIVE REPETITIVE REPETITIVE REPETITIVE REPETITIVE
REPETITIVE REPETITIVE REPETITIVE REPETITIVE REPETITIVE
REPETITIVE REPETITIVE REPETITIVE REPETITIVE REPETITIVE
REPETITIVE REPETITIVE REPETITIVE REPETITIVE REPETITIVE
REPETITIVE REPETITIVE REPETITIVE REPETITIVE REPETITIVE
REPETITIVE REPETITIVE REPETITIVE REPETITIVE REPETITIVE
REPETITIVE REPETITIVE REPETITIVE REPETITIVE REPETITIVE
REPETITIVE REPETITIVE REPETITIVE REPETITIVE REPETITIVE
REPETITIVE REPETITIVE REPETITIVE REPETITIVE REPETITIVE
REPETITIVE REPETITIVE REPETITIVE REPETITIVE REPETITIVE
REPETITIVE REPETITIVE REPETITIVE REPETITIVE REPETITIVE
REPETITIVE REPETITIVE REPETITIVE REPETITIVE REPETITIVE
REPETITIVE REPETITIVE REPETITIVE REPETITIVE REPETITIVE
REPETITIVE REPETITIVE REPETITIVE REPETITIVE REPETITIVE
REPETITIVE REPETITIVE REPETITIVE REPETITIVE REPETITIVE
REPETITIVE REPETITIVE REPETITIVE REPETITIVE REPETITIVE
REPETITIVE REPETITIVE REPETITIVE REPETITIVE REPETITIVE
REPETITIVE REPETITIVE REPETITIVE REPETITIVE REPETITIVE
REPETITIVE REPETITIVE REPETITIVE REPETITIVE REPETITIVE
REPETITIVE REPETITIVE REPETITIVE REPETITIVE REPETITIVE
REPETITIVE REPETITIVE REPETITIVE REPETITIVE REPETITIVE
REPETITIVE REPETITIVE REPETITIVE REPETITIVE REPETITIVE
REPETITIVE REPETITIVE REPETITIVE REPETITIVE REPETITIVE

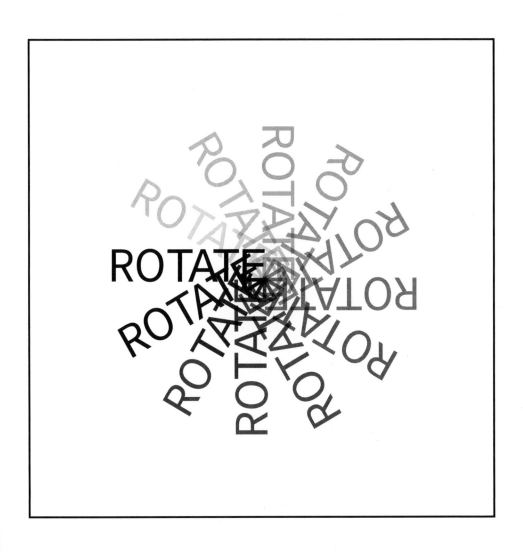

S GR GAT

E   E   E

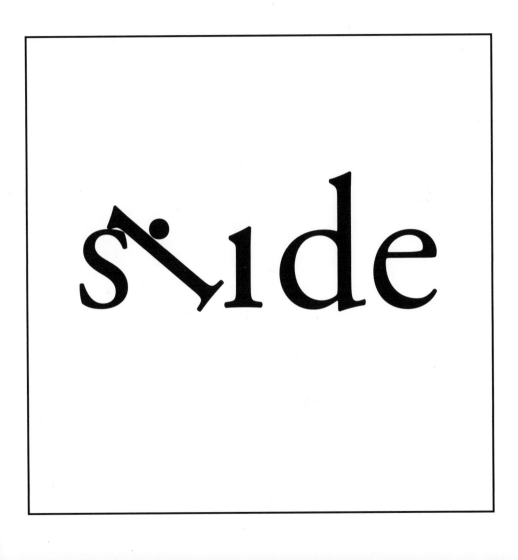

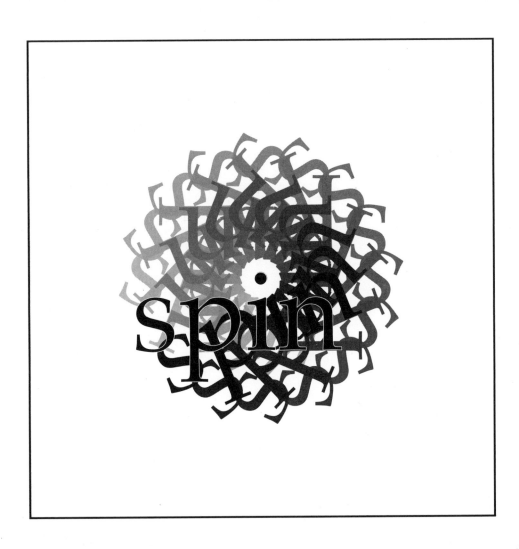

STENCIL

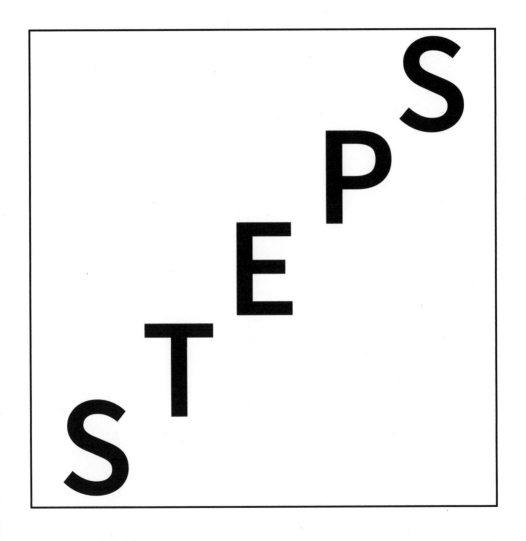

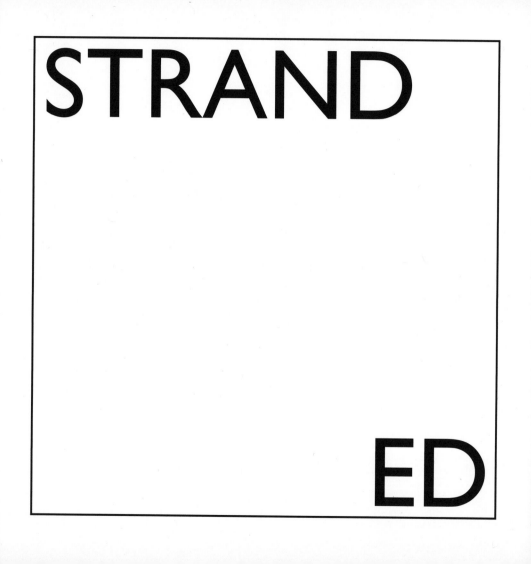

STRAT STRAT STRAT
| | | | | | | | | | | | | | | | | | | | | |
FY FY FY FY FY FY FY

SUBST1TUTE

SYL · LA · BLES

SYMMETRICALLACIRTEMMYS

ASYMMETRICAL

TANGENT

TRANSITION

trivial

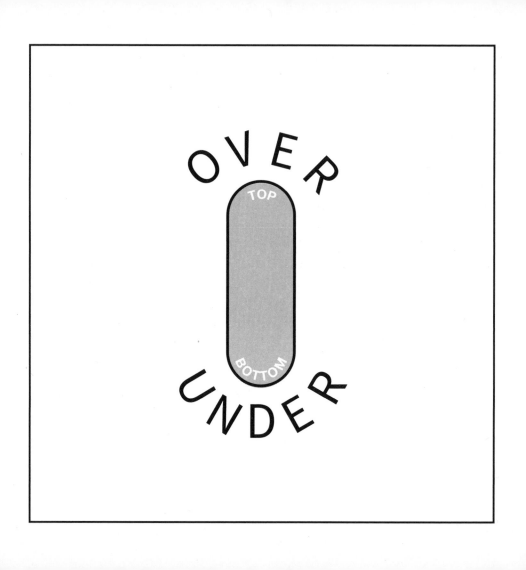

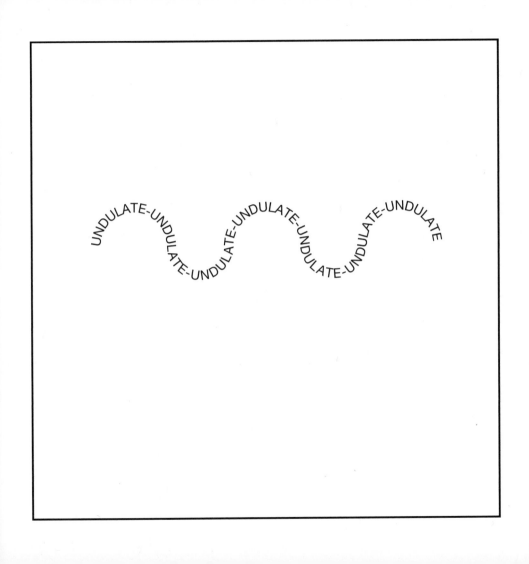

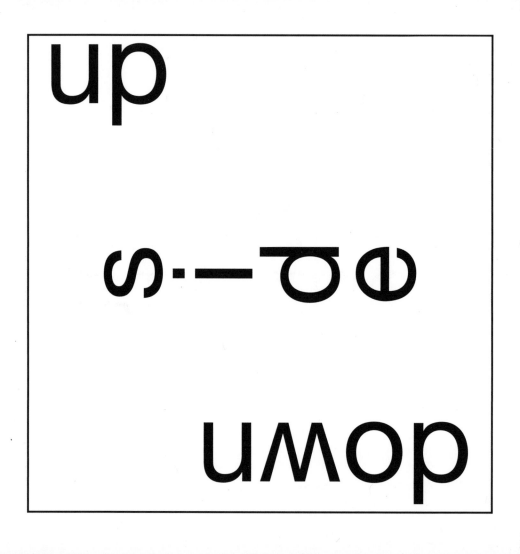

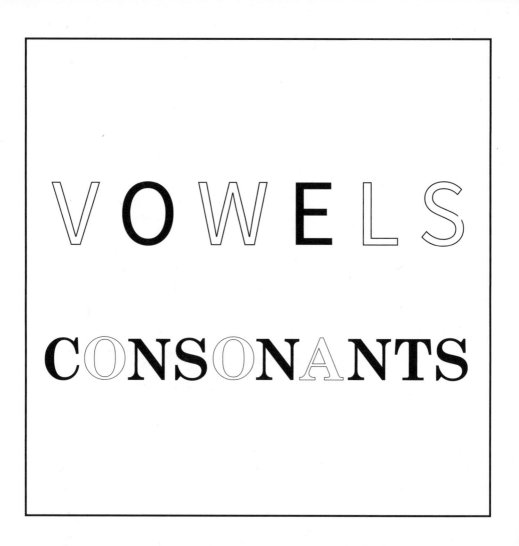

HALF

WHOLE

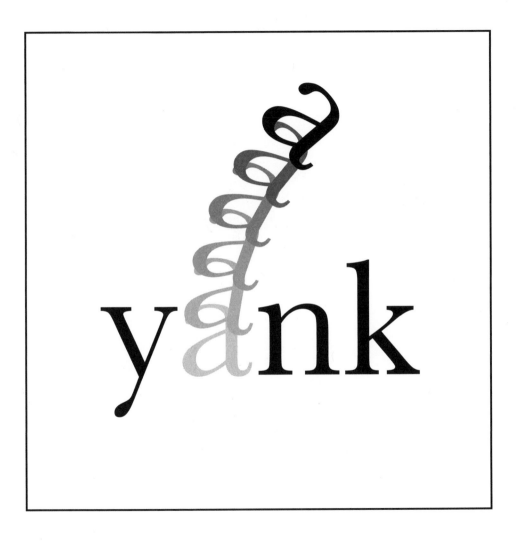

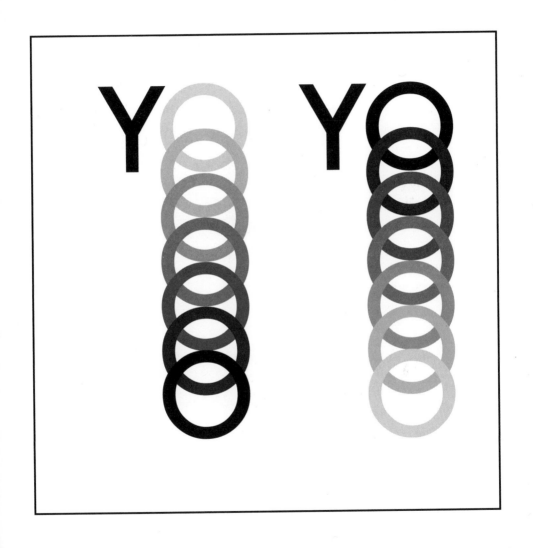

Cover design by Michael Pause
Type set in Helvetica Neue LT Pro / Proxima Nova

ISBN: 978-0-7643-6452-5
Printed in India

Published by Schiffer Publishing, Ltd.
4880 Lower Valley Road
Atglen, PA 19310
Phone: (610) 593-1777; Fax: (610) 593-2002
Info@schifferbooks.com
www.schifferbooks.com

For our complete selection of fine books on this and related subjects, please visit our website at www.schifferbooks.com. You may also write for a free catalog.

Schiffer Publishing's titles are available at special discounts for bulk purchases for sales promotions or premiums. Special editions, including personalized covers, corporate imprints, and excerpts, can be created in large quantities for special needs. For more information, contact the publisher.

FSC
www.fsc.org
MIX
Paper from responsible sources
FSC® C016779